PORTRAIT OF
THE ISLE
of WIGHT

Ian Badley

HALSGROVE

First published in Great Britain in 2009

British Library Cataloguing-in-Publication Data
A CIP record for this title is available from the British Library

ISBN 978 1 84114 957 8

HALSGROVE
Halsgrove House,
Ryelands Industrial Estate,
Bagley Road, Wellington, Somerset TA21 9PZ
Tel: 01823 653777   Fax: 01823 216796
email: sales@halsgrove.com

Part of the Halsgrove group of companies
Information on all Halsgrove titles is available at: www.halsgrove.com

Printed and bound by Grafiche Flaminia, Italy

INTRODUCTION

From my early years, when I was fortunate enough to live overlooking The Needles, albeit from some distance away, I have always found the Isle of Wight to be a fascinating place – so close and yet so far. Often I would watch as the clouds appeared to hang over the island, providing an additional dimension to its bright chalk cliffs. Occasionally, mist would swirl around its shoreline producing an ethereal effect on the scene. Its misty valleys and coastline still attract me now. The diverse coastline, from rocky outcrops and high cliffs in the west to the vast sandy beaches in the east which are favoured by families with their buckets and spades, always provide photographic interest. Yachting, an intrinsic part of island life attracts many hundreds of thousands of visitors a year and boosts the economy commensurately. The Isle of Wight gives the opportunity to view and photograph this sporting and leisure activity from close quarters. For walkers and photographers alike, inland, the downs of the island provide stunning vistas and a healthy activity into the bargain. With its historical places such as Carisbrooke Castle, the Town Halls of Brading and Newtown together with the strategic and interesting towns of Ryde, Sandown, Ventnor, Newport and of course Cowes, one never tires of the island. Full of fascination and, from my point of view, photographic opportunities, I have endeavoured to illustrate some of these in this book. In compiling and researching this book, I have found out interesting facts and discovered wonderful places that I didn't know before. Exploration whether close to home or as a visitor, broadens your mind. The Isle of Wight achieves that objective in spades.

Ian Badley

LOCATION MAP – Isle of Wight

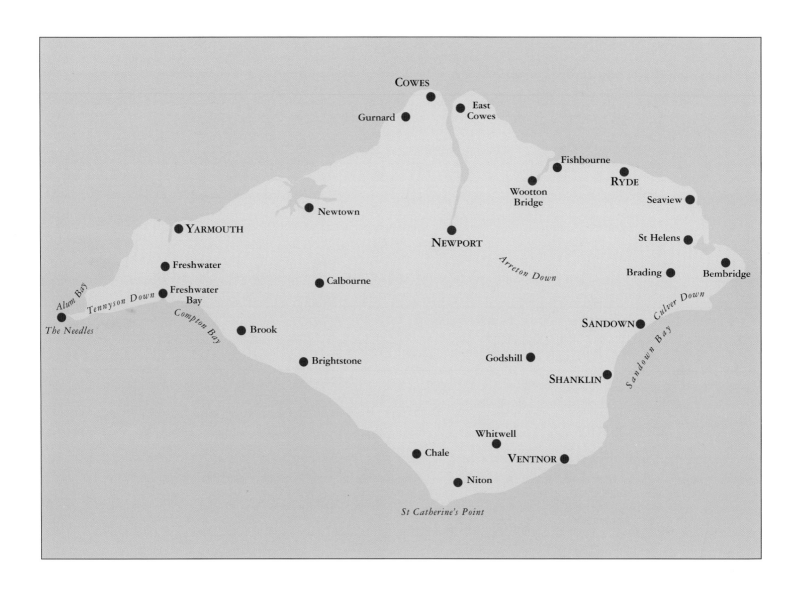

Wisteria surrounding a cottage doorway in the picturesque village of Calbourne.

Heavy clouds over the island producing squally showers.

A colourful sky at dusk reflected in the wet sand on the beach at Hanover Point, on the west of the island.

Right:
An abstract image of the waves far below Tennyson Down on the west of the island.

Right:
Sheep grazing on Mersley Down with low lying mist in the early morning, looking out towards Fishbourne and the mainland beyond.

Left:
The Isle of Wight coastal footpath at Culver Down, looking towards Sandown on one of the bright sunny days with which the island is synonymous.

Left:
Pennant flags on the stays of a classic yacht moored in Yarmouth harbour for the Old Gaffers yacht regatta. The Old Gaffers regatta draws yachts from far and wide and usually runs annually.

Right:
Tall sailing yachts making way through the western approaches of the Solent during the annual Round the Island yacht race.

Above:
Sunrise looking out over the mist-shrouded River Yar valley
to the sea beyond.

Left:
Fishing boats on trailers adjacent to the pathway to Brook Bay, on the
western coast of the island.

Above:
Looking out towards Niton Down over hay bales lit by early morning light and mist covering the valley floor.

Right:
Sandown Bay across the mist covered River Yar valley streaked by early morning sunlight. In the distance you can see a large ship anchored.

The monument to the Earl of Yarborough on Culver Down. Charles Anderson-Pelham, was the 1st Earl of Yarborough (1781–1846) and the founder of the Royal Yacht Squadron.

The view out to sea
over Culver Cliffs.

The windmill at Bembridge, a
Grade I listed building and the
last remaining windmill on the
island.

Green beach huts reflected
in the rock pools at Bembridge.

Lobster pots on the quay at Yarmouth with the ferry berth at dusk. Yarmouth is a busy local port for fishermen, visiting yachtsman and the thousands of visitors using the Lymington to Yarmouth ferry.

Looking from the sand dunes on The Duver, into Bembridge harbour as the first golden light of sunrise strikes the grasses on the dunes.

Striped deck chairs on the beach at Shanklin, with people swimming in the sea and paragliders in the sky.

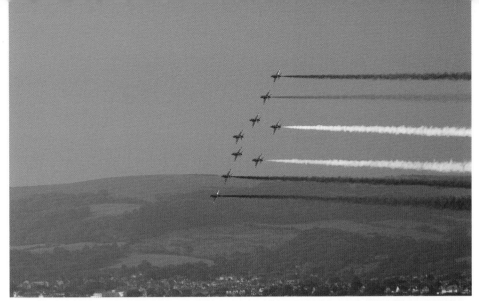

Left:
The Red Arrows in formation above Sandown. Standing on Culver Down provides a magnificent view of these skilful acrobatic pilots.

Below:
Fields at dawn shrouded in mist with Knighton and Sandown beyond.

Sheep fields near Roughland Cliff.

Art Deco-styled flats at the entrance to Cowes harbour.

Weed-covered rocks at low tide on
Brook Bay as the sun sets.

Two sheep grazing on Mersley Down with low lying mist in the valley beyond.

The lifeboat station jutting out into the sea at Bembridge.

A warm setting sun lights the yellow cliffs which are reflected in the rock pools at low tide. Here you can see the strata in the cliffs and many people look around the beach here for fossils.

Looking into the hull of a traditional clinker-built wooden sailing boat.

A couple walking along the beach at Compton Bay, at low tide with a colourful sunset.
The dip in the cliffs behind them is Freshwater Bay.

Left:
Mist in the valley by
Rowlands Wood.

Right:
A colourful sky at dusk
reflected in the wet sand
and rock pools on the beach
at Hanover Point, on the
west coast of the island.

Above:
A fishing boat leaves Bembridge harbour at dawn.

Right:
The quaint beach huts on the promenade at St Helens near Bembridge, which were converted from old railway carriages a good few years ago now, provide an interesting diversion from the norm.

Looking out towards Sandown Bay with wild flowers in the foreground and mist streaked with sunlight in the valley of the Yar River Trail near Newchurch.

A fisherman walking towards his fishing boat moored at Bembridge harbour.

Above:
Looking across fields of corn at Crouchers Cross way before dawn.

Left:
First light on moored yachts at Bembridge harbour. All along the
shore lie house boats painted in bright colours.

Above:
Colourful beach huts on The Duver at St Helens.

Left:
Low tide at sunset with a view towards the
coastguard cottages at Brook Green

St Helen's Old Church on the sea front on The Duver at St Helens, was built around the fourteenth century and later painted white to act as a marker for boats at sea.

The Causeway, running from St Helens, across the Mill Ponds to The Duver, an area for birds and wildlife, backing onto the sand dunes of The Duver.

Above:
A colourful sky after sunset, reflected in a large rock pool with
two fishermen standing on the beach at Compton Bay.

Right:
A yacht resting on its keel at low tide on the rocky shoreline of Seaview.

A dinghy lying on wet sand at low tide at Seaview.

Cyclists and cars using Ryde Pier. The pier which has been extended a number of times is over 600 metres long. Originally it was built in the early nineteenth century to serve the town of Ryde and is still in active service now, providing a regular access point for boats to Portsmouth. In addition to being extended, it has also been widened sufficiently to allow cars to drive along it in both directions at the same time.

The view towards Ryde over mist covered fields with Spinnaker Tower, Portsmouth in the distance.

The ruins of the Cistercian abbey near Quarr Abbey, Ryde.

Looking down Wootton
Creek from the weir at
Wootton Bridge.

The church at Godshill from
the remembrance garden.

Looking towards the white cliffs of Tennyson Down from Stenbury Down.

The lighthouse at St Catherine's Point at the southern tip of the island. This distinctive octagonal-shaped tower now provides a marker to ships in the English Channel. Records show that there has been a light here since the fourteenth century.

Hay bales drying in fields on Niton Down.

The view over Brighstone out to sea from the Worsley Trail on Brighstone Down.

The entrance to the fort of Carisbrooke Castle, nestling on the hilltop to the south of Newport. There has been a settlement here since Saxon times, although the current castle was built around the eleventh century. Charles I was famously imprisoned here in 1647, from where he tried unsuccessfully to escape.

Two cannons on the hillside battlements of Carisbrooke Castle. It would appear that after the Spanish Armada came close to the island the cannons were placed strategically to provide further reinforcement to the castle.

Silhouetted trees on Ventnor seafront against an austere sky.

The entrance to Ventnor harbour, showing the fishing dock with lobster pots and hoist. Here the catch of crabs and lobsters is weighed before being sold on to restaurants on and off the island.

The winding staircase
of the pavilion on
Ventnor seafront.

A jet ski riding through the waves off Sandown beach.

Above:
A lone yacht makes way below dark storm clouds with shafts of sunlight off Ventnor.

Right:
Late afternoon sun lights Brook Church and Brook Hill House, with dark storm clouds beyond. JB Priestley lived at Brook Hill House in the late 1940s having moved there from nearby Chale Green.

Left:
The view to All Saints' Church at Godshill with the famous thatched cottages surrounding the green in the foreground.

Right:
Looking out to the chalk cliffs of Freshwater Bay from the coastal footpath at Compton Chine.

The view south from Compton Down along the coastal footpath towards St Catherine's Hill.

The last light of the day on the cliffs of Freshwater Bay with pink hues on the clouds in the sky.

Above:
Sunrise on the creek at Newtown, Isle of Wight, showing the wild ducks and
an egret wading at low tide. Newtown Creek is a National Nature Reserve
owned predominantly by the National Trust.

Left:
The historic Town Hall at Newtown lit by the first sun rays of the day.
Newtown was formerly known as Francheville and dates back to around 1300.
It was an important borough on the island until the nineteenth century
when it was declared a 'Rotten Borough' and later disenfranchised
under the Reform Act.

Above:
Camp Hill, one of the Isle of Wight prison blocks viewed through the trees from nearby Parkhurst
Forest. There are three prisons in the same area, Parkhurst and Albany being the other two.
Until recently they used to be high security prisons incarcerating such infamous characters as
Ronnie and Reggie Kray and Peter Sutcliffe the Yorkshire Ripper.

Left:
Early morning light on the walls of Carisbrooke Castle taken from the vantage point near
Whitcombe Cross.

An early morning view across to Gatcombe, which was recorded in the *Domesday Book*.

Looking over the rooftops to the river entrance at Cowes.

The lifeboat slipway at Freshwater Bay after sunset with a dark cloudy sky.

A close up of a ship's propeller from HMS *Cavalier* standing at Cowes Esplanade looking out to the Solent. HMS *Cavalier*, a destroyer, was launched in 1944 and decommissioned in 1972. She was built by JS White and Co on the island using new welding techniques to make her faster in the water. She now lies at Chatham Dockyard in Kent.

A yacht sails past Cowes town on the River Medina towards the moorings on a bright autumn morning.

The chain ferry crosses the River Medina at Cowes, linking East with West Cowes. The ferry, or floating bridge as it is often known, was launched in 1976 and carries over 1.5 million foot passengers free each year. It operates 365 days per year and the short journey takes only a couple of minutes. Around 400,000 cars and vans are also carried across at a fee.

Fields at dawn shrouded in mist with Knighton and Sandown beyond.

Top:
One of the many posts depicting Cowes placed around the town.

Left:
The last light of the day on the cliffs of Freshwater Bay with pink hues on the clouds in the sky.

Right:
An abstract picture of one of the modern high rise buildings built on the Cowes waterfront.

Right:
One of the many pubs in Cowes and an alleyway leading down to the waterfront as a ferry steams by. Cowes is linked by ferry to Southampton which is one of the routes used to bring the millions of people who visit the island each year.

Left:
The landing stage for royalty in front of the Royal Yacht Squadron at the entrance to Cowes harbour. The landing stage is directly outside of the Royal Yacht Squadron Headquarters which was originally built as a castle by King Henry VIII in the sixteenth century to protect the island from the French.

One of the famous cannons used to start the many hundreds of yacht races that take place each year during Cowes Week.

The balustrade on the landing stage in front of the Royal Yacht Squadron.

The rusting remains of the *Ryde* paddle steamer now in decay on a River Medina boatyard. The *Ryde* was commissioned in 1936 and served during the war in the North Sea and as part of the D-Day landings before being used again as a pleasure craft on the island.

Top:
The carved statue of a bull commemorating the historic Bullring in Brading, where bulls were once baited by dogs. Brading – believed to be derived from its historic name, Brerdynge – used to be a major port on the island, until the river silted up many years ago.

Left:
An abstract view of the hull of a yacht, dry berthed on a River Medina boat yard.

The busy quayside during Cowes Week with sailing yachts racing in the background. Cowes Week has been a part of the British sporting heritage since 1826. The event usually takes place during the first week of August and brings many thousands of visitors to the island together with yachtsmen from all over the world.

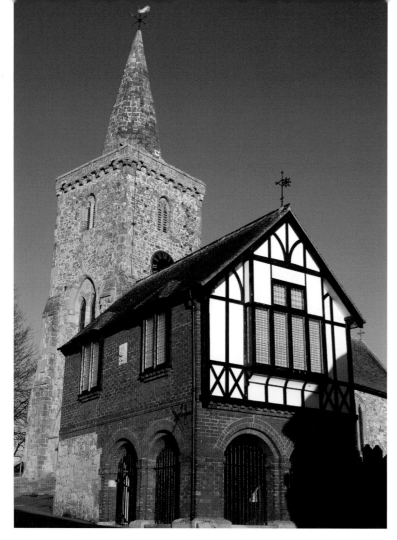

Top:
The old Town Hall with its stocks and church at Brading. The town
was given a Royal Charter as long ago as 1548 by Edward VI but there
has been a settlement in the area since Roman times.

Right:
The colourful sands in the cliffs at Alum Bay, with Hurst Castle and
the Western Approaches to the Solent beyond. The coloured rocks and
sands are the result of geological folding many millions of years ago,
causing the various strata to lie vertically as opposed to horizontally.

Moored boats on the River
Yar at Yarmouth at dusk.

Top:
The Harbour Master's launch on the River Medina at
Cowes. In busy summer months, he stands station to
advise yachtsmen on where berths are available. Owing to
the vast number of visitors, this can be a daunting task.

Right:
A busy evening at the yacht marina in Cowes. The sheer
numbers of visiting yachts to the island and in particular
Cowes, makes for a tight squeeze with many yachts being
moored up to five abreast.

Top:
Three yachts racing off Gurnard in the Solent.

Right:
A fisherman on the beach as yachts contesting the Round the Island race pass by.

Top:
Sails and masts of a closely contested class of yachts vie for position at the start of a Cowes Week race.

Right:
Colourful spinnakers on yachts racing down the Solent during Cowes Week.

Looking up to the windmill at Bembridge.

Stormy skies and a rainbow over the ferry
terminal at Cowes.

A classic yacht sails out of the River Medina at Cowes past the
Harbour Master's launch.

Yacht masts in the marina at Cowes, showing how tightly packed they are in this crowded haven for yachtsmen.

A melange of boats in the Solent during Cowes Week. This image was taken from the shore off Egypt Point at Cowes with the action taking place around 100 metres from the shoreline. Egypt Point is a popular grassy viewpoint for Cowes Week yacht racing.

A moored sailing yacht in Newtown Creek
before dawn with mist rising.

Top:
An abstract composition of colour and graphic lines from one of the
beach huts on The Duver, complete with resident spider.

Left:
Sunrise over the dunes at The Duver, St Helens, Isle of Wight.

Top:
Dinghies on the shore at Fishbourne. Fishbourne, at the
mouth of Wootton Creek, is another of the ferry ports
linking the island to the mainland.

Right:
A fishing boat at anchor in the Solent off Seaview.

A yachtsman working on his yacht at one of the boat yards adjacent to the River Medina. With yachting being synonymous with the island for many years, it provides a vital income source to the island's residents and economy.

A stile on Stenbury Down looking out across fields towards Ventnor and the sea beyond.

Top:
Flags and masts in Yarmouth harbour during a regatta.

Right:
Crashing waves and a late afternoon sun looking
out to Sandown Pier. The pier was built originally
towards the end of the nineteenth century and rebuilt
a number of times since.

Left:
Picturesque Winkle Street in Calbourne Village.

Right:
Looking over to Tennyson Down with people walking towards the Tennyson monument, high on the eponymous downs. Alfred Lord Tennyson was born in 1809 and moved to the island with his wife around 1852, living near Freshwater until he died in 1892.

A crewman tightens the sheets of the sails on a classic yacht off Yarmouth in the annual Old Gaffers yacht race.

The bow of barge competing in the annual Old Gaffers yacht race in the Solent off Yarmouth.

Right:
Looking out across rough seas towards Castle Cove near Ventnor.

Top:
Three teenagers playing on the groynes at Sandown.

Left:
Dinghies at Seaview sailing club.

Top:
A dinghy lying on wet sand at low tide at Seaview.

Right:
Fishing boats, cabin and lobster pots on the promenade at Ventnor.

Left:
A setting sun over Tennyson Down viewed over exposed rocks at low tide from Hanover Point.

Right:
A rural farmhouse near Whitwell.

Stenbury Down looking over fields of hay bales to the coast.

Walkers on a footpath adjacent to hay bales on Niton Down.

The entrance to Carisbrooke
Castle.

An Isle of Wight ferry, hydrofoil and yacht at the busy entrance to Cowes harbour.

Fallow deer in a field near New Close, Newport.

Top:
The name plate on the renowned marine photographers Beken of Cowes. Alfred Beken moved to the island in 1888 when he purchased a pharmacy. Fascinated by the many yachts racing he attempted to photograph the spectacle but found it very difficult. He designed his own camera using two wooden boxes which were joined for use and held in his hands. To fire the camera, he used a rubber ball connected to the camera by a hose, which he bit to expose the shot.

Right:
Colourful picket posts on the seafront at Ryde with the Spinnaker Tower at Portsmouth in the distance.

A cannon at the entrance to the Royal Yacht Squadron, Cowes.

PRIVATE LANDING PLACE
FOR MEMBERS OF THE R.Y.S.
AND OFFICERS ENGAGED ON
HER MAJESTY'S SERVICE

Left:
The Royal landing stage in front of the
Royal Yacht Squadron at Cowes.

Right:
Blue doors on one of the sail lofts at
Cowes.

The stocks under the Town Hall at Brading.

Looking out onto the Solent through the arches under Victoria Fort on the north coast of the island.

Looking along the coastal path past a Yarmouth lifebelt over the harbour to the town and its church beyond.

The view down the water taxi pontoon onto the harbour and Yarmouth town with its church beyond.

Top:
The blue bell at the entrance to Yarmouth Pier. Yarmouth Pier, built of wood in the late 1800s,
is over 650 feet long and as such is the longest timber pier in England still open to the public.

Right:
A picnic table amongst the tall pine trees of Parkhurst Forest.

Left:
The quayside at Newport harbour at the head of the River Medina, with a colourful sky dotted with puffy white clouds. Newport harbour lies some 5 miles inland from the sea on the River Medina. At low tide it dries out completely. Newport is the County Town of the Isle of Wight and centre to the island administration.

Right:
Sail and motor boats moored on the quayside at Newport harbour.

Top:
Looking down river at Wootton Bridge to the moored boats.

Right:
The bridge over the River Yar at Yarmouth at dusk. It is thought that the
Celts made a settlement in Yarmouth, then known as Ermude, meaning
muddy estuary, before the Romans. Now it is a bustling yacht haven,
working fishing port and ferry terminal for vehicle and foot passengers to
Lymington on the mainland.

The clock tower
on the theatre at
Ryde.

An image of Ryde Pier taken from a different perspective, illustrating its length.

Admiring the view during
the Old Gaffers yacht regatta
based in Yarmouth.

The town name of Ryde painted onto a colourful clinker-built boat on the gardens at Ryde seafront.

Looking back to Ventnor
from the sea wall.

The view across to Hurst Castle on the mainland from the coastal footpath above Fort Albert near Freshwater.